FROM FISHING TO TUMBLEWEEDS

A Journey of Life, Death, Grief, and Faith

Debbie LaFe' Fordyce

ISBN 978-1-68570-482-7 (paperback)
ISBN 978-1-68570-483-4 (digital)

Christian Faith Publishing
832 Park Avenue
Meadville, PA 16335
www.christianfaithpublishing.com

Printed in the United States of America

CONTENTS

To MOM AND DAD, FOR their story, and my husband, Roy, for his support.

INTRODUCTION

HAVE YOU EVER WALKED THROUGH the *end-of-life* journey with a friend or a loved one? In this story, you will find how Father and I traveled the road together. It's a glimpse of what might happen, and how faith plays an integral part in planning for and traveling the end of life. You will get to see the emotions Father and I experienced as well as the preparations we did or did not do. We had faith in each other, but faith in God was ultimately the biggest factor and cannot be discounted at any cost.

Included are some tips and encouragement to use in your own end-of-life planning. While I am not a financial guru, I have experienced helping Father with my mom's end of life, plus being power of attorney during Dad's last years and then a successor trustee after death. End-of-life and estate planning are valuable tools that give you fewer things to worry about when your emotions are running high. I have worked with financial advisors, an attorney, tax advisors, a CPA, home caregivers, nursing homes, assisted living, hospice, funeral homes, insurance companies, stock portfolios, realtors, bill collectors, and banks.

If you are thinking about how this all might look, I implore you to examine our experience to see if some part can be applied to your own planning. While no one's journey is quite the same, this book may give you things to think about and a glimpse of this stage of life.

CHAPTER 1

FAMILY LIFE

THE CALL

I CAN STILL REMEMBER THE scent of fall in the air as the phone rang, jarring me from my book as it fell to the floor. The assisted living where Daddy resided was calling to warn me that he might not make it through the night. That call had come several times in the last few months, but lifting my heart to the Lord, asking for His presence, seemed the right thing to do. Struggling to keep my emotions in check, tears ran down my face, making me dab at my eyes. About an hour later, the phone rang again while shivers in my neck and back created tension throughout my body. Drawing a deep breath, the phone was answered again with the message that it was finally over. Upon hanging up, there was a burst of sobbing and tears that prompted my husband to console me.

This call had not been unexpected but rather a long time coming. I was now an adult orphan, and there was a great feeling of loss, but relief was also mixed in. Why was I relieved? Daddy was gone, the man who shaped my life, taught me lessons of how to not only survive but also to live joyfully, fully, and to be curious. Concentrating on myself was not what he taught me. I needed to do better. Thinking in a self-centered way, guilt washed over me. Again, relief came into my thoughts along with memories of the more than

1

two years of struggle. Trying to stand, knees trembling, I prayed, *Dear God, give me the strength to move forward in what I now must do.*

My thoughts drifted to Mom and Daddy running through a field of yellow poppies toward each other, like the commercials of young lovers on TV. Pretty good visualization for a couple in their nineties, don't you think? This was not the beginning or the ending, so maybe I should take you back a spell to share our story.

WHERE MOM AND DAD CAME FROM

Mom grew up in a large family and was born in 1922 on a family farm in Georgia. She had one sister and four brothers, in addition to a brother who died as a toddler. Mom was next to the youngest of her siblings and lost her father to an illness as a young teenager. My grandfather, Jerome, had worked on the family farm but eventually moved to Tampa, Florida, for better opportunities. He had been quite ill over the years with smallpox, then typhoid fever, and suffered greatly from those diseases. Not many people in the 1930s survived one much less two such devastating illnesses. He made it through both, but his health was not the best.

His death left the family without much money, so the kids all worked to help support the family. Even as adults, all the kids took turns living with Grandma Rachel, to keep her financially afloat. Mom's homelife was strong during adversity, exhibited great faith, and had kindness and love in abundance.

Daddy, on the other hand, was pretty much an only child born in Tampa, Florida, in 1920. He did have a half-brother, but he never talked much about him. I assume there must have been a wide age gap with no real closeness. Daddy often got into trouble as a youngster, according to my grandmother Edna, but he took responsibility for his actions.

Once, Daddy went to the swamps in Florida, where he wasn't supposed to be, and got bit by a water moccasin. He got himself to a doctor and made payment arrangements. He was just a young boy of about nine, who was trying to hide his disobedience from his mom. Dad's teenage years brought the young man who got expelled from high school for throwing castor-oil beans from the balcony at other students below. Again, he hid it from his mom, but according to her, she knew of both situations anyway. She didn't punish him, that I recall, but she let him suffer the consequences.

Dad's father left the home around the time of the Great Depression in 1929. This left Daddy and Grandmother with no real income. Nanny, as we called her, was married five times, trying her best to provide for Dad, and later his younger brother. Dad said there was always a new man around to boost the family finances, but they lived with relatives between marriages. In those days, marriage was sometimes the only way to survive economically for a small family. For this reason, Dad gave her credit as she lost a couple of husbands to death.

OUR FAMILY BEGINS

The notion of our family began when my mom Margaret and dad Gene met through mutual friends. Daddy was enamored immediately with what he considered a beautiful woman with a great personality. He believed her to be quite spectacular and surely out of his league. Mom, on the other hand, really wanted nothing to do with Dad. He was good-looking but short and very much a pest. If it had not been for their friends, Mom may never have considered linking up with him at all. With that said, I once asked Mom what made her change her mind about spending time with him. The answer was, "He more or less grew on her."

Dad in his later years confirmed for me that it was definitely an uphill battle, but he had no intention of ever giving up. They were married for seventy-two years, so I guess Dad won that war. They truly loved each other through all of life's grand and devastating times.

When Mom (eighteen) and Dad (twenty) married, they had to get permission from their parents because they were under twenty-one. They had a small wedding at Grandma Rachel's house with just family, having an outdoor reception in the yard to include friends. Spending their wedding night at Mom's brother and sister-in-law's house, they then went on a short honeymoon trip. Upon their return, they lived for a while with Grandma Rachel.

Daddy worked for a dry cleaner and then with the railroad. Both jobs paid little but put food on the table. Mom spent time working at a dime store temporarily. In those days, the norm was for only single women to work outside the home while a housewife was to be at home having babies. Times have certainly changed, haven't they? He tried to enlist in the United States Army before WWII, but they were quite selective until after Pearl Harbor. By the time the war had started, he had decided on the United States Navy, feeling it was a better choice. Dad, being a patriotic man, enlisted in 1942, which gave them a small but steady income. Once that decision had been made, he liked the benefits, so he began a career of twenty-four years.

My sister Karen arrived on the scene as the first child. Dad was stationed in Washington, DC, but Mom went to Florida so Grandma Rachel could help when my sister was born. Dad had to stay in Washington, DC, on orders, but I am sure he was very excited. It's my understanding that he was so happy to have his first child that he gave her a form of his name to be included in hers. This started an awesome tradition in her line of descendants of passing on the name.

Almost six years later, I entered the picture when the family was living on the Great Lakes Naval Training Center in Illinois. This time, there would be no grandma to help as she had passed away less than three weeks before I was born. Mom had been having a difficult pregnancy and had been forbidden by her doctor to attend Grandmother's funeral in Florida. She tearfully wrote her siblings about her dilemma, but I think she may never have gotten over it. I think she always felt guilty as the waterworks would start up just talking about it. The doctor had given Mom strict orders to stay home, and Dad enforced them. So I guess my birth was a sad time yet ended on a happy note.

At my birth, Mom and I got to enjoy a few extra days in the hospital because Dad and Karen broke out with chickenpox. Whew! Must have been the start of sibling rivalry! What a great beginning to life I had, causing all that turmoil. I know it wasn't funny, but it makes me laugh just thinking about the two of them covered in spots.

MEMORIES OF CHILDHOOD

Our family was a loving one, and I remember taking vacations to various places like Cape Canaveral, James Town, Disneyland, and Sequoia National Forest just to name a few. We traveled a lot when Dad had leave (time off) from the military, and I have many fond memories of the trips around the United States.

Dad liked to take home movies, so he always had a camera in hand and kept some of those early films to the end of his life. Since we did all these vacations in the car, Mom was always equipped to fix a picnic lunch of canned lunch-meat sandwiches. Sometimes I thought she must have been on the company's payroll as the sandwiches on white bread were a staple at our house. I was always car sick on those vacations or just on our Sunday afternoon drives, but I enjoyed them anyway. Sunday afternoons were like a scheduled family car ride. We got to see lots of cool sites, including huge waterspouts over the Florida waterways. Those trips, both long and short, were special days, and our parents did the best they could to expose us to nature and fun.

A very vivid memory I have of Dad's loving care and gentleness was when I fell into a tumbleweed. I was about six and had an abundance of spines sticking out all over, looking like a dog who tangled with a porcupine. What a sight I was to behold. Daddy carefully got me home and began the process of pulling them all out. He took the initiative to get the task done before Mom got home. I wasn't any worse for the experience but knew that Daddy loved me. Falling into this tumbleweed began my association with all the thorns that life throws your direction.

Life, in the navy brought a lot of challenges for our family. Serving from 1942 to 1967, Dad was gone from home a great deal. If memory serves me correctly, he missed my first five birthdays. I remember there were times when I was afraid that he would forget who I was, but he always remembered. It's crazy what a small child will imagine, and I was no different in that department.

While we missed him being home, he did everything possible to make it up to us. Usually, this came in the form of special presents and lots of attention. I enjoyed the many gifts such as a big red bike, a miniature tea set in a blue box, and a baby doll from Japan. The bike got stolen, I kept the tea set until it disappeared in a move, but I still have that baby doll. Dad would spend quality time with each of us girls doing things we each liked, such as fishing, the movies, or Sunday afternoon family drives.

To this day, I refuse to bite my nails as Daddy once made me sit all the way through a movie on my hands for biting them. He asked me once toward the end of his life how come my nails always looked so nice, and I reminded him of his punishment. He got a real kick out of the story and how it affected me. While he didn't remember the incident, he said it struck him as something he would have done.

With our homelife revolving around Dad's military career, Mom was part of the Officers Wives Group, which helped her reputation as a spectacular hostess grow. Unlike so many in the service, there were no alcohol or smoking habits in the family. This helped provide Dad with a continual clear head, allowing him to zero in on his work without distractions. Both Mom and Dad gave up so much of their freedom to serve our country. Dad always had to leave while Mom took up the slack at home. We lived in rentals, our own homes, and military housing while moving from place to place. Mom and Dad both told me that he stayed in the military so long because he wanted to give our family the stable life he never had, as well as his patriotism.

I often thought of Dad being one of the smartest men alive. Not sure if it was my imagination that made me think so or what because he had a limited education. At any rate, I was impressed, and I trusted his instinct in most areas. As I was growing up, Daddy would often tear apart the television, while the family was at church, to eliminate lines or shadows that no one else could see. In fact, Dad put together our first color television from a kit. Quite a chore for the average person I would think.

Forty years after building that TV, he still had the old television tubes in the garage. It took the garage burning down in a wildfire to get rid of them. He was quite the collector of objects and gizmos. I can remember that when home computers became available, he would often dig into programs to see how they worked. He was a problem-solver with a big impact. This allowed him to do the work necessary to receive a commendation from the secretary of the navy. I think this was the one thing he felt most proud of during his career. What an honor for both Daddy and the family!

My sister and I were given opportunities that other children might not have had. We were often invited to go fishing on military charters, had a family rowboat, and my personal favorite was to fish off bridges. My sister was able to catch a sailfish on a military charter while I was seasick below deck. While we all fished in the rowboat, Karen went mostly on those journeys due to my motion sickness. I spent quality time with Dad individually, fishing the waters of Florida off bridges. Not sure how much fish we caught in the long run, but the experience taught me that Dad wanted to spend time with us.

Daddy had been fishing since he was a child in Florida, which I am sure contributed to his always fishing for knowledge. Because of the military life, we moved a lot but were forced to learn how to adapt to new places and friends. I loved all the new adventures, and to this very day, I have a desire to move about or make changes every few years. We were often allowed to go on dependent cruises, which were awesome by the way. It was great to feel the ship skim over the water, but the best thing was to experience a little of Dad's other life. There are too many opportunities to mention here, but I for one loved the military life.

When I was a teenager, I was able to join the Junior Army-Navy Guild Organization as a volunteer nurse's aide. It was like the old candy stripers, only at the military hospital. This was during the Vietnam War, so perhaps I saw a lot of things most teens are protected from. The following is a true experience I wrote about because of the lesson it taught me:

The Eyes

As I entered the sky bridge, I saw two men at the far end heading my way. Drawing closer I noticed one was a corpsman, the other a patient in his hospital

7

issue robe and slippers. The corpsman was my friend Robin, so we greeted each other as we came side by side. Robin introduced me to his charge, a young Marine. What I saw as I looked him in the face made my stomach uneasy. His face was pitted with black spots that were left by mortar rounds. His eyes I will never forget as they were fixed wide open. The color was black with no whites, like you would see in horror movies. As he faced me it felt as if he was staring right through me which made me very uncomfortable. I heard a small child's voice yelling, "Daddy" from behind me. As the child came closer, I saw her with eyes wide open, reaching to grasp the man beside me. A child that could only see the man she loved and respected. Not the ugly remnants of raging war. This child taught me that we have to look beyond the obvious and examine what lies behind our immediate circumstances. (2011)

This is also something Dad tried to teach us. He looked at what made things the way they were rather than what was apparent on the surface. I imagine this idea was why he spent so much time tearing apart the TV or investigating a computer program for the inner workings. As an adult, I can now see that teaching in how I react to most everything. I always want to look beyond and try to figure things out. I am never satisfied with the unknown and must fish for knowledge. I am sure it sometimes drives people crazy, especially my family.

With Dad being in the military, life always had a sense of danger, but that danger was never talked about in our home. Mom was a strong woman of faith and tried to help us concentrate on our daily lives rather than fear. We did, of course, have times when we did worry about his safety but were taught to place our faith in God and keep going.

I do remember two specific times when I was afraid during Dad's absence. One was when I was about five or six, and I worried that Dad would forget who I was and what I looked like. Nine months is forever for a child, and I was no different in that respect. The other was when he was in Vietnam. He had to move a lot from hotel to hotel because of his expertise in the scheme of things. The hotels, for some reason, kept blowing up behind him, giving me the distinct feeling he was being chased like James Bond. Perhaps the danger was less than I thought, but with my teenage mindset, I was deeply afraid. His job was a very important one, and the enemy knew it. I remember wishing he would come home *now*.

I wrote the following from some diary notes I had from the time Dad was in Vietnam:

The Hotel Diaries

Dear Diary,

Today is Friday, and we didn't receive our weekly letter or cassette tape from Dad. I guess the mail must be slow this week. I mean, after all, the letter is coming from halfway across the world.

Dear Diary,

It's Saturday, and we still haven't heard from Dad. What's the scoop? Mom says don't panic, he is probably just busy and couldn't write this week.

Dear Diary,

Dad's letter is another week late today. We heard on the news that the Viet Cong are blowing up hotels in Saigon. Mom's not sure what hotel he is in since he moves often. Is Dad all right?

Dear Diary,

We got a letter today, and Dad says he is okay! It took two weeks to arrive so the mail must be really slow. He named the hotel, but I can't spell or pronounce it. I sure am glad he is okay!

Dear Diary,

Just heard on the news that the hotel Dad said he was staying in was blown sky high! Is Dad hurt? Is Dad dead? God protect my daddy!

Dear Diary,

It's been two weeks since the newscast about the bomb. We still haven't heard from Dad. The military hasn't contacted us so maybe he is okay, but I am really worried.

Dear Diary,

Dad sent a telegram today, and he is okay. Yahoo! I am so excited. He got out about ten minutes before they blew up the hotel. I wish Dad would come home. I am really scared!

(2011)

In Dad's military career, he served during World War II, Korea, the Cuban Crisis, and Vietnam. With all that war, it could be thought that he would be a worrywart about safety yet with a tough exterior. However, as I grew up and after becoming an adult, his favorite words to me were, "There you go worrying yourself again." He was a mild-mannered man, but you knew when he meant business. Monkey business was not his forte, yet he had a great sense of dry humor. Not many people understood his funny side, but I found it refreshing.

As you can see, my father was a family man and loved each one of us without reservation. He seemed to be making up for the lack of true family life during his own childhood. He was not a traditionally religious man but had the morals and attitudes of one serving Christ. Dad had a terrific sense of doing what he thought best for his family. He instilled a deep work ethic in my sister and me, plus he took time to relax and build relationships. Mom, on the other hand, was the ultimate homemaker. She was bold yet strong and presented us with a superb example of depending on your faith in God. Between the two of them, we had a well-rounded life that most kids today can only dream of.

When I married, my husband asked Dad for my hand in marriage. I know that seems corny to today's generations, but that was how it was then. My dad's reply was that he didn't see any reason why not. This was quite a concession on his part because Daddy being navy had trouble with the idea that Roy was an air force man.

It was the age-old rivalry between services that became a teasing bone of contention between them. Dad always thought I married the wrong service. Those two were quite comical about the subject. I am sure there were times that Dad wondered if I had made a mistake, but by the end of his life, they truly cared for each other. Daddy often told me that I should keep him. Those two were quite the pair from my viewpoint. I know Dad was very appreciative of all the time that my husband gave up for me to come down and for all the things Roy would do for him.

CHAPTER 2

LOSING MOM

Mom's Declining Health

Mom's health had been declining for a few years, yet I chose not to think it was more than age affecting her. I really didn't think that she was close to the end of life even though she was ninety years old. She had suffered from early dementia for a couple of years, but she still made sense most of the time. A while before she died, I mentioned to Dad that he should have her mental state looked at as I had really noticed changes. He said he hadn't noticed, but I think maybe he just didn't want to. I don't think he really wanted to acknowledge that she was struggling. About a year or so later, she had a seizure and fell. She was transported to the hospital ninety miles away. After some testing and several days of hospitalization, she was sent home under hospice care. Dad was under the assumption that he could take care of her as he had in the past. He didn't understand, at this point, what hospice meant in the scheme of things.

When he found that he couldn't really care for her, my sister and the hospice nurses helped him to understand that she needed additional care. I had been there to spend time with her and see how things were going, so I agreed that the money needed to be spent. Living in a rural area, she was placed in assisted living where hospice could assume responsibility for her medically, and Dad could visit every day. It was just down the street, and the owner was friends with my parents.

I visited her a few times during the next six weeks, but since I lived five hours away, it was difficult to make the trip as often as I wanted to. Suffering great guilt of not being able to see her more often, I retired. This allowed me to spend more time with her while I could. This was a sacrifice financially, but sometimes family must come first. My sister lived in another state, so it was impossible for her to come often. Mom and Dad's friends did visit her on a regular basis, but she seldom remembered they had been there as soon as they left. I am sure she felt loved anyhow even if for only a fleeting moment.

Every day, she would ask Dad if he was going to take her home that day, and of course, he had to respond, "Not yet." It was hard on him, and it broke his heart, yet he continued to visit daily. Having been married for seventy-two years, he was quite used to having her around and often ate lunch and dinner with her at the facility. Dad kept believing that she would get well, but it was not to be.

A few short weeks after my retirement, Mom took a turn for the worse and went on to be with Jesus. Dad called from her room as it was happening, and I could hear the hospice chaplain, their pastor, and others singing hymns to her. One of the friends got on the phone and said, "You better come." So I quickly packed a bag, contacted my sister, and headed out the door. The usual drive seemed to take forever, but it was actually faster as I was preoccupied. With all the traffic and my thoughts elsewhere, I feel God must have protected me on my journey. The whole time I was in turmoil and praying that she would still be alive when I got there.

After arriving, I found that she was gone. I had missed saying goodbye and was devastated that I had missed her last moments. The woman who I loved, who was my best friend, who prayed for me, and who led me to the Lord was gone.

Feeling guilty for not being there for Mom's final moments, I found Dad at home alone. He was sitting in his chair, waiting for me to show up. He kept saying, "I didn't know she was going to die. I didn't know" (LaFe, Gene). Now I prayed that God would give me strength as it was clearly not the time for me to break down. I missed

Mom terribly as she was a joy giver and my support system. Mom had a habit of speaking loudly with her actions in the likeness of Jesus.

I will be forever grateful that she was the one who shared God's word with me, giving me the opportunity to come to know and build a relationship with Jesus. As Dad and I hugged, the tears flowed, but I was acutely aware that he needed me to be his support system, his right-hand woman so to speak. I could never fill Mom's shoes but would strive to be his arm to lean on. After chatting for a little while, he passed the reins to me to get everything accomplished.

The Struggle of What to Do

Well, there I was with Dad, struggling, and I had no idea where to start the process of the arrangements or what anyone wanted. Luckily, Mom had left a file that gave me some clues of what she might want for her funeral. Other than that, I had no idea what to do. So I made a list of things I could think of and got going.

My sister, being in another state, was too far away to help with details. My husband was still at home taking care of things there, so I enlisted our dear friend Clara to aid me. I will be forever grateful as Clara was a godsend to me. I put aside my grief as much as I could and attempted to stand strong for Dad who was totally in a daze. Without my faith in God, I would have surely crumbled under the pressure. Dad could not help with the arrangements, so I had to be responsible for the decisions. Acting like a well-oiled machine to get things done was a challenge. I thank God for keeping me focused.

I had never planned a funeral before, so I was floundering under the emotional strain. Putting my emotions on hold, I avoided totally breaking down. Dad, Clara, and I drove to the funeral home to make the arrangements. It was quite emotional, and it took a lot to keep from crying when Dad would occasionally wipe a tear. Keeping strong helped the choices to be made as Daddy was there, but not really present, if you get my drift. We made decisions based on what looked like Mom, keeping Dad's money output reasonable.

I found the funeral director personally wonderful. He had worked with Mom and Dad on two other occasions, making the situation more bearable. My parents previously opted to be cremated as they wanted to be buried at the military cemetery. That was the only type of option left in that location, so the decision was simple. Dad and I also met with the church pastor who knew them well. He had requested that we find a scripture that Mom loved, which was hard because she loved it all. She had been in the habit of writing in her Bible, so I found a comment that spoke to me about how she felt. The comment that stood out was, "God really knows all about me" (LaFe, Margaret). The comment was handwritten next to the following scripture in her Bible:

> *O Lord, you have searched me and you know me.*
> *You know when I sit and when I rise; you perceive my thoughts from afar.*
> *You discern my going out and my lying down; you are familiar with all my ways.*
> *Before a word is on my tongue you know it completely, O Lord.*
> *You hem me in—behind and before; you have laid your hand upon me.*
> *Such knowledge is too wonderful for me, too lofty for me to attain.*
> *Where can I go from your Spirit? Where can I flee from your presence?*
> *If I go up to the heavens, you are there. If I make my bed in the depths, you are there.*
> *If I rise on the wings of the dawn, if I settle on the far side of the sea, even there your hand will guide me, your right hand will hold me fast.*
> *If I say, Surely the darkness will hide me and the light become night around me, even the darkness will not be dark to you; the night will shine like the day, for darkness is as light to you.*
> *For you created my inmost being; you knit me together in my mother's womb.*

> *I praise you because I am fearfully and wonderfully made; your works are wonderful, I know that full well.*
> *My frame was not hidden from you when I was made in the secret place. When I was woven together in the depts of the earth, your eyes saw my unformed body. All the days ordained for me were written in your book before one of them came to be.*
> *How precious to me are your thoughts, O God! How vast is the sum of them! Were I to count them, they would outnumber the grains of sand.*
> *When I awake, I am still with you. (Psalm 139:1–18 NIV p. 741–742)*

It was a little unusual for a funeral, but it spoke volumes about Mom and her faith. She truly believed that God knew all about her and cared enough to be an integral part of her life. I believe this faith made her the strong woman she was. The pastor was able to build his words around it, and I'd like to think the whole thing really spoke to us as a family.

Following Mom's service, we had to begin thinking about what was next. Mom had been ninety years old while Dad was ninety-two at the time. He was sure he could still live on his own with a little help from Clara, so the decision was made to let him try. Mom had been concerned that if she went first that he would become a hermit. With that thought in mind, she had made both Clara and I promise her individually that we would take care of him. Whew, what a request!

It was challenging to take care of someone who wanted to be independent. How do you have trust that he would not be too lonely, uncared for, or depressed? I was scared about the process but knew I needed to depend on God completely. Clara and I did manage to get through it, becoming better friends than ever. While not a sister by blood, Clara had been a great friend to my parents over the years. They thought of her as their adopted daughter, and she thought the same.

CHAPTER 3

CARING FOR DAD

NEEDING MORE CARE

DAD STAYED HOME FOR MORE than a year, but the pressure of daily life had mounted. I was beginning to see the strain on him build, with each trip I took to see him. He no longer wanted to be in control of things yet didn't want to give up his control either. Dad and I began to forge a bond that would only tighten and never be broken. He started telling people to ask me about things because he didn't want to think about them.

When Dad became confused on a regular basis, we, as a family, began thinking about a more suitable situation. His hours became mixed up, and sleep patterns were out of the norm, making eating and taking medications haphazard. Clara was diligent about fixing meals, preparing his medications, and so forth, but Dad would forget even if they were sitting in front of him. He sometimes had difficulty telling what was real and what wasn't.

I had been asked to come to stay for a month while Clara was on vacation, so I packed up and moved in for a while. I took over Clara's duties plus continued with the finances I was already doing. Of course, I had to assist my husband in any way I could from a distance, so I was losing stamina quickly. Often Dad would sleep off and on for eighteen out of twenty-four hours and then be awake at night. This made me quite tired just watching him.

While taking up roots at Dad's place, I became pretty much emotionally drained. It was disabling being away from my husband and all the support he gives me. I was missing my friends and normal activities. Still attempting to avoid grieving for Mom, fear crept in of becoming a basket case. How could I be useful to Dad if I allowed myself to break down? Trudging on, a new sense of determination seeped in, of keeping my promise.

Not all the days were stressful as there were times when all seemed normal and good. I was able to really talk to Daddy about every subject imaginable. He loved a specific news channel, and so it was on twenty-four-seven. While Daddy and I had similar political ideas, enough is enough! It's sad when you know all the news people in a twenty-four-hour period by first name. Oh my, and the TV volume was loud enough to be heard around the world. Of course, we won't discuss the heater levels that made him comfortable while I could barely move without sweating.

In some regards, it was a joy to spend quality time with him, but I missed my husband terribly. It was a challenging time for us as a family. Watching Daddy decline was extremely difficult. The once mentally alert man was now sleeping the little time he had left away. I cried a lot when alone, while frustration and sadness set in. Watching him fail created a lot of fear that I would not be strong enough to endure the process, yet in my heart, there was the knowledge that God alone would get me through. Thank you, Jesus, for your ever faithful presence!

During his stay at home, Daddy had visiting nurses, physical therapy, and, of course, the ever-increasing trips to the doctor. The process of keeping a daily log of behaviors exhibited began, so they could be shared with his medical team. Occasionally, the notes were shared with him but not always. The way he would perk up and hide his condition when they would visit was a little scary because he would then sleep excessively. He didn't want them to know how he really was, but they guessed anyway. With the logs, they had a clear-cut picture of behavior that he refused to show to anyone but me. Feeling like a tattletale, I never discussed what was happening in front of him. The medical team was quite concerned about his condition, and the need to be hospitalized arose several times.

THE CHOICE OF HOW TO PROCEED

Finally, the time came when we were able to convince Dad that he needed more medical care and that it wasn't fair of him to burden Clara with it as she was still holding down a job. So my sister planned a visit and found a facility that could meet his needs. I had been there for thirty days, so I needed to return home for a few weeks. My sister got him to agree to be admitted to a nursing home at the hospital, following some dangerous things he did due to his medications, age, and general condition.

Originally, he had wanted to go to the same place where Mom had resided, but they did not have room for him at the time. We did promise him he could go there when they had a room. I was thankful my sister was able to get this accomplished and felt the burden ease for myself and probably Clara as well. This began the journey of still making him feel wanted and needed. I think Daddy felt like he might have been thrown to the wolves at this point, and that's probably normal for most people. The time had come to concentrate on making him feel loved and confident that he was still important to us all.

About six months into his stay at the first home, some changes took place. Dad was declining medically, and the home was closing. So a new place had to be located in a hurry as we were only given thirty days. Yikes, I am so glad God opened the door at the location where Mom had been. We took advantage of that open door, making a swift transition to what is affectionately called the "Casa." This was to be Dad's new home for the remainder of his life, which was about two years. I was able to visit every five or six weeks for a few days, staying down the street at his house. While the trips were exhausting, they helped keep things under control.

In Dad's new residence, he began to thrive again. Not sure why exactly, but it was a more home-like atmosphere than the first location had been. The number of residents was reduced, and so was the number of caregivers. It was less like an institution and more like a home with medical benefits. Here, Dad was valued as a person and started to rally. Family was welcomed to spend time there and even eat with the residents on occasion.

I met some workers there who will remain part of my life forever. The owner/manager became a family member, watching out for Daddy. The two of them had a very special bond that has lasted even after his life. He often gave ideas and plans to her that could improve things overall and even helped financially with some of them. One of these ideas was a system that would assist both patients and caregivers to have better communication from a distance. The caregivers were wonderful, and Dad was extremely fond of them. It was like a real family with love and quarrels yet total respect for each other. How awesome to have that personal touch in an assisted living scenario. I was so glad that God had blessed our family with this living arrangement.

Daddy had been placed under hospice care at the assisted living and his visiting nurse, Virginia, and the chaplain, Brian, played a big part in his medical, emotional, and spiritual care. Daddy told me the story of his nurse singing hymns with him when she visited. I had never heard Daddy sing before, so I was impressed that she got him to sing along. Virginia and I became good friends and still have an ongoing relationship to this day. She made this end stage of life easier with her love and care. She and Daddy often discussed the spouses they both had lost, and how proud of them they were. Virginia, for her husband's accomplishments, and Dad would visualize Mom and the beautiful way she carried herself. Virginia has expressed how much Daddy loved Mom and us girls (Smith, Virginia). I believe that these conversations gave Dad a friend to rely on over time.

Dad appreciated the hospice chaplain Brian so much that he requested him to play a part in his funeral service. They used to have long conversations about life and spiritual matters. So by the time Daddy left us, they had a meaningful bond. Even after Dad was gone, the chaplain and I did some grief therapy, which really helped me to heal. Overall, the assisted living process leading up to the last days was a good experience for all of us. Daddy was able to pass through the tumbleweeds of life with dignity and knew he was loved and appreciated.

Over the last two years of life, we began discussing Dad's wants, needs, and how best to get through the journey. Everything I did financially for him was talked about. It somehow seemed important that he could be involved in financial decisions for as long as possible. A habit grew that I would do what was necessary and then bring the bank statements or other important items for him to view what was done. Even though I was doing it all beforehand, he could still be in the know when it came to everything. Daddy loved spreadsheets so that is what he got in abundance. Not that he read them all, but he was appreciative that I prepared the information for him. Building his self-esteem was important to his well-being. It made him relax and know that I had a handle on his affairs.

Daddy eventually began to realize that the end of his life was coming, and things needed to be set in place to make the journey easier. As I watched him failing, I would talk with him for hours about what he wanted. Medically, he wanted to do as much as possible for as long as he could. Financially, he didn't want to make decisions but gave me input when needed, which kept him in the loop. He had set up a living trust after Mom had passed to make matters after death easier, and while I knew nothing about them or how cumbersome they can be, I am grateful. It spelled out his wishes at the time.

We started the discussions of what he wanted in a funeral and who he wanted to take part. I opened a file like Mom had done for her funeral service but included all his financial dealings as well so things would not be missed. Each of these items was discussed to gain any knowledge he could provide. I found it time well spent when he was gone.

It was important to me to make sure that Daddy knew Jesus like I did. As I mentioned before, he was not a traditionally religious man but exhibited signs that indicated he might be a Christian. He had not gone to church with us as a family, but I know he went with Mom at times during their marriage. He often told me that he was looking forward to seeing Mom in heaven. I decided the best tactic was to stop stalling and come right out with the question. So I did. Joy filled my heart when he assured me that he did have a believer's relationship with Jesus. I am so glad I asked him! My heart would be at peace at least on that subject.

When Daddy was alive and able to communicate effectively, I felt I had an ally in the process. Once he was gone, this feeling faded, and thoughts of abandonment crept in. It took real diligence of daily talking to God to allow myself to feel comfort in God's presence. My Lord and Savior was there all the time. I just had to open the door and let him in. I prayed:

> *Oh, Jesus, let me feel your comfort and know that through you I can do what it takes to finish the task you have set before me. I praise you, Lord, thanking you for your presence! I know your word says that you are my strength and will guide me through my turmoil to a more blessed faith in you. I trust you, O Lord, and will do my best to follow your ways in all my dealings. When I falter, I ask your forgiveness, knowing you are the One True Living God. As I give my earthly father over to you, I pray that you will accept him into your glory, and you will comfort all who knew and loved him. Thank you, Jesus, for being there for me. (August 2017)*

CHAPTER 4

THE WHIRL ZONE

WHERE HAS MY MIND GONE

NOW WE HAVE COME FULL circle back to the original call. Daddy was dead, and what is left of my family was once again fractured. My mind was going crazy. I couldn't do the task. My mind was spinning, and I kept thinking in illogical patterns. What was I to do first? Crying was all I could manage while my emotions were running so high. It had only been a short span of time since I lost Mom, and now Daddy was gone too. I couldn't breathe, trying again and again. I asked the Lord to help me. I couldn't do this by myself. My husband put his arms around me, and instantly I was comforted. My breathing slowed to normal, but the tears continued to flow. I know I should have taken out stock in a tissue factory. I would be rich by now!

Beginning to regain my composure, my mind drifts to the time Daddy and I spent preparing for this moment. We had realized after Mom's death that important decisions should be discussed before the emotions go wild. No one likes to discuss the impending end of life, but I believe that the momentary discomfort can be worth it when the time comes. We had made lists, talked about feelings, plans, and most importantly what Daddy wanted to be done with his estate. I had reminded Dad that everything he had was by a joint effort with Mom over the years. Therefore, it was important to con-

23

sider what her wishes might have been as well. I found it so much easier emotionally to go down my prepared list of things to do than to have to think. I truly wanted to be more organized and efficient than normal. This wasn't a time to be unsure about anything. We had planned, discussed, and agreed on how things were to be handled. So time to get going and make it happen.

Making things happen quickly and efficiently is easier said than done. The mind is so boggled with a mixture of loss and guilt and overwhelmed by the fact that the funeral service will not be the end. In my case, there were still a couple of years of financial dealings to get through, and the paperwork is endless. I had been Dad's power of attorney before death and the successor trustee of his estate afterward. I was well acquainted with his finances, but there was so much to do.

I praise God that we had done some estate planning ahead of time. I can only imagine how hard it would have been had we neglected that or if death had come quickly before we could talk about things.

PREPLANNING A SERVICE

After my personal experiences with end-of-life dilemmas, I would like to persuade you that every family should talk about how they perceive this process. I know some will refuse to discuss the subject thinking that it can never happen to them; but in reality, it happens to everyone. Death comes in many forms and at inconvenient times. Of course, it is easier to plan with old age or extended illness, but accidents or other things can happen tragically and leave you in the whirl zone for an extended time. Therefore, I believe it is important to have at least preliminary discussions when everyone is healthy and safe. It can be as simple as making a file for each member of the family with their favorite music, colors, flowers, charities, and who could potentially talk or sing at their service. This is a good time to declare the choice of cremation or burial and what kind of place they would like to be interned.

Families, and individuals within a family, will have different ideas about this subject. This can be a family project, and any information in the files can be altered with time as desires change or simply left as is. While not a legal file, it can be a step to recognizing a person's likes and dislikes. The file Mom made was extremely helpful in expressing things she thought were important. This one step can save thousands of dollars in planning a funeral because snap decisions can be made with unclarity of choice expressed. How does a person want to be remembered? This is the question.

The planning of a funeral generally comes when the family is in the whirl zone. Emotions are running high and cloud good judgment. We are all fair game when it comes to grief. We all experience it, reacting differently and at separate speeds. It is extremely difficult to make sound decisions about budget and where and how at the last minute. I would recommend putting funds aside in a savings account because it is all quite costly. I am sure you have seen all the commercials about the expense of funerals, and they aren't kidding. However, a lot of money can be saved by preplanning and sticking to a budget. Not all services have to be done with the best of everything and riches galore. It makes no difference to the one who has gone on and only leaves the survivors in debt. Careful preplanning plus taking an individual's desires into consideration is quite helpful.

There are many things to think about in planning: flowers or donations, location, music, speakers, and obituaries to name a few. A good funeral home might be able to help with details, so they aren't forgotten. It can be a valid field trip in preplanning to visit your local mortuary to see what services they provide and get potential costs. This can help you set up a budget while your mind is clear.

After Mom's funeral, Dad went to the local mortuary and said, "I want a funeral just like my wife's, and I want to pay in advance." So that was accomplished. Although his service was slightly different and at another location than Mom's, the major decisions were already made and off the table.

If you are using a church for the service, be sure and talk with them about any requirements and fees associated with the location. Check online for the types of services and what to put on your list.

Every person's list could vary depending on the budget. Throw things you like in your prep file, and I think it will make decisions easier when you are under duress. Also, as an additional thought, put a pack of *thank you* notes in the file to thank people for those meals they drop by. While you may not feel up to it, common courtesy improves your disposition.

CHAPTER 5

SURVIVORSHIP PLANNING

MAKING A LIST OR TWO
AND OTHER TIDBITS

MANY PEOPLE HATE LISTS, BUT when it comes to getting through all the financial debris, I highly recommend them. To stay organized, I started with a basic list and then branched out from there. My dad had a living trust, which stipulated how things were to be divided, but that doesn't really take care of getting things closed out so you can divide them. Don't let anyone fool you. It is a lot of work.

In my case, I spent two years before the final taxes were filed and the funds disbursed. With the trust, we were able to avoid probate, but we still had to have two sets of taxes: one for the individual and one for the trust. As an average person, there was no way I could do it alone, so I hired a CPA. Some people use tax attorneys or other professionals well versed in estate taxes. This is important because the laws can change, and the average person might have trouble keeping up. I certainly did.

Because Daddy trusted me, he placed me on his bank accounts and safe deposit box, so I would have easy access to funds to pay any bills before and after his death. After death, I opened both a checking and savings in the name of the trust to keep funds coming in from insurances or other financial accounts separate from the bill-paying accounts. For funds coming in, I needed a trust EIN (employee identification number) to use instead of his social security, which you need to apply for. This was quite confusing, yet if you make notes that make sense and stay on top of things, it helps.

Some people hire a professional to do all this hard work, but of course, I floundered alone. I did use the financial advisors at the bank to help with opening those trust accounts and got a lot of valuable info from them. There is also a lot of information online and some great websites to help guide you. If you could even possibly be the person who will handle everything, do some research and ask for help from professionals.

One thing I found that maybe you might want to investigate is this. Daddy made me his power of attorney before he died, so I could handle financial matters for him as needed. In most cases, all I had to do was send a copy to a company, and I could do whatever was needed. I did run into one company that refused because he was not declared incompetent. They required documentation for that item. So my advice is to have the attorney word the power of attorney to say that you can act without having to make those declarations. Dad never was incompetent. He just didn't want to be bothered with the frustrations of business. After death, all I had to do was send a copy of the trust and the death certificate, and I could do anything.

Mom and Dad, over the years, had increased their life insurance, creating over ten policies with the same company. This was a nightmare. Most did not have documentation except for the dividend checks. It took a long time to blaze this trail as the company had split, and some went one way and some another. It was quite a challenge to navigate all of them as even the company had issues. Don't give up, and ultimately the goal can be reached, but it may take time.

Some insurance policies and annuities had beneficiaries designated, and some did not. My sister and I had to do our own paperwork on some items, and others went straight to the trust. Keeping track was the hardest part. If the funds are being split into multiple directions, I truly advise making sure beneficiaries are designated when insurance and annuities are started. It will save a lot of headaches later.

Of course, my way is not the only answer. I am just sharing what worked for me and what didn't. The following are examples of lists that were helpful to me, but I urge you to do your own research for important information that changes over the years. Time changes laws and processes. These ideas are only to give you a starting place.

1. A list of bank accounts and numbers, insurance policies, annuities, investment accounts, and any other financial information: This includes social security numbers, date of birth, date of death, and EIN information. Every place I talked to required the information. Be prepared to spend hours on the phone, calling places to report the death. Be sure to collect information on how to proceed to close things out. Being in the know is better than regretting mistakes because you did not ask a question. Also, order lots of copies of the death certificate as you need them for everything. I think it is better to have more than you need than to have to reorder.

2. A list of what is in a safe deposit box if there is one: Always keep a list at home and in the box itself that is continually updated with additions and deletions. Get everything out before closing this account. It can be tricky if you are not a signer on the safe deposit box, so it is good to get that done before death. My dad trusted me not to steal anything, and I know some families may not have this relationship. I had no problem because I was a signer and able to access the box at any time, but others may not have this advantage. I would recommend talking to the bank or attorney for information on procedures if you are not listed on the safe deposit or bank accounts. A big recommendation here is to prove yourself trustworthy to your family. It has the potential to solve a lot of issues.

3. A list of people to contact about the death including phone numbers and addresses if possible: I didn't have this and had to go through old address books looking for information. If you find one person, you can ask them who else they think might like to know and how to reach them. I contacted one cousin I had information for, and she gladly contacted other families in her part of the country. I also asked someone at the church to contact people who would want to know.

4. A list of credit cards and other recurring bills that might need to be paid, such as utilities: It's important to keep up with the incoming bills. Don't let things lapse, or you could end up with late charges or cancelations. Don't forget to check in the cushions of furniture as sometimes important stuff is stuffed there for later. In our case, Dad had a supply of old mail stuffed in his recliner. Also, go on a hunt for loose change around the house in strange places. We ended up with several hundred dollars in change that was just put in drawers and various containers in unexpected places.

5. Keep notes of calls and correspondence in a notebook: Everything you do needs to be documented, including the time you spend on it. I would write down dates, time, who I spoke with, what was discussed, and phone and fax numbers and emails. I also had the habit of writing down with each conversation what the next step was. This helped me tremendously. Remember to keep records of your time spent as a trustee or other given title so you can legitimately pay yourself from the estate. Plus, this must be counted as income and reported on all the taxes involved. This makes it critical to have a tax advisor of some kind.

SELLING PROPERTY

Selling property can be just a headache or a downright disabling crisis. I was fortunate in that my sister and I both agreed that we would sell the property. Neither of us really wanted it but could have bought out the other person if we did. As the trustee, I had the authority to sell for any reasonable price, but I felt it important to consult my sister before agreeing to any offers. The property really wasn't worth a lot in our opinion, and I think we were both glad to get it off our hands. Many families fall apart in arguing over property, so if it can be sorted out beforehand, you will be better off. Grief and greed seem to go hand in hand for some individuals, and I praise God that we didn't have that issue. Daddy had made it clear in the trust that everything was to be split into equal shares, making any decision easy and fair.

Now comes the challenge of what to do with all the belongings in the house. There was a lot, considering Mom and Dad had lived there for over forty years. I had put off doing anything until after death because Daddy would often ask for something, and he knew right where it should be. Since there were only two of us, we talked about what we each would like to have, and luckily it wasn't the same list.

My hubby and I went through everything in the house and took multiple trailer loads to the dump of trash and unusable items. We gave some items to the church youth group for a fundraiser they were having and some special items to our dear friend Clara plus other families. Then we called a local auction place that came and got everything else for an auction at their facility. We didn't make much money, but at least it was gone. Even the ragged cat-torn sofa was sold, so I was surprised. Using the auction process saved us from having to do a garage sale in a rural area. The idea of all the work in handling a garage sale didn't appeal to me even a little bit. Do some research in your area of what might be the best option for you.

Then came the huge chore of cleaning the empty house. All in all, things went smoothly, yet it was a tremendous amount of work. I would have totally been at a loss without my wonderful hubby, who is the one you want around if you need to get something done. He has more batteries stored in his system than most people, so I will forever be grateful for his willingness to help.

In some locations, homes sell slowly, and that was the case in our area. Sales were taking close to a year in most cases because it was a rural place. The property was a doublewide-manufactured home on five acres with the garage having the most value. Due to the age of the home, it had to be a cash offer, making us question how soon we would be done. It was in fairly good shape, however, and the new owner bought it sight unseen.

I would say, we were blessed because it went quickly and easily. I also give credit to our real estate agent who made things go smoothly. He was able to help out with things that were hard for us because of the distance. I did have to make a trip for the closing, but that was okay and gave me great relief that it was over. All I had left to do on this was divide the profit as the trust stated.

Keeping the Faith

When Jesus spoke again to the people, he said, "I am
the light of the world. Whoever follows me will never
walk in darkness, but will have the light of life."

—John 8:12 (NIV p. 1331)

In Mom's Bible, I found a handwritten note that said, "Grief stays with us always. It just moves over a bit so we can deal with the rest of life" (LaFe, Margaret). I am not sure if this was her thought or if she got it from a sermon somewhere. Obviously, it struck her as something to remember, and I want to give credit to whoever originated it. I stand in agreement with this statement as grief changes how it affects us over time but never really goes away. I still grieve for both my parents, yet as time has gone on, how I react to that grief has changed. When it was fresh, I either stood strong or tearful and afraid. Now I am taken back when certain memories crop up, yet I can focus more on the ideals they taught me and the love we shared.

There were so many times I fought to stay on track and not give up. I set up a lantern to represent Mom and Daddy still shining in my life. This gave me peace that I would always have them in my memories. The task of staying on track was hard but survivable. How I would ever find my way through the turmoil escaped me. Turning to God was not a crutch for me. It gave strength to carry on because of his ever-loving grace.

I must say I give the most praise to my Lord and Savior Jesus Christ for all he has done for me personally. I know that sounds preachy to some people, but it is truly heartfelt. Without my relationship with him, my journey would have been devastating. Instead, he gave me strength to follow through and Dad the strength to endure. I was told following Dad's death that he had asked for a suitcase before he died. That they were waiting for him (Lara, Iliana). He was ready to join Mom and Jesus, as we used to say.

Thanking You with Praise

Thank you, O Lord, for coming into my life and for saving me from my sinful nature.
You have played such an important part in the way I strive to live my life.
I know that you are always there for me and will never push me away.
Although I have sometimes wandered from your guidance,
I continue to find myself returning to your waiting arms.

Lord, you have provided me with guidelines for daily living,
Always anticipating the needs that I will have.
You experience my joys and sorrows with compassion and love,
Completely sharing all the emotions with your caring heart.

Jesus, you are a friend on who I can depend, as well as my savior and Lord.
I thank you for the daily adventures you bring to my life,

Making me learn about compassion, trust, love, and commitment.
I worship and praise you, O Lord, for who you are.
(Deborah Sue Fordyce, May 2000)

Epilogue

For me, the true definition of fishing is not just a means of finding food. It revolves around the process of questing for information and knowledge or enjoyment. It's the unquenchable desire to know the inner workings of everything life brings your way. In the same way, tumbleweeds are not just a bush that breaks off and tumbles around scattering its seeds. A tumbleweed is how life moves us around, bringing invasive thorns that prick your emotions and thoughts. They give you cause to stumble and break apart yet make you stronger than before. Ultimately, everyone's life goes from fishing to tumbleweeds, from the beginning to the end.

For God so loved the world that he gave his one and only Son,
that whoever believes in him shall not perish but have eternal life.

—John 3:16 (NIV p. 1320)

BIBLIOGRAPHY

New International Version, Disciple's Study Bible, Holman Bible Publishers, Copyright 1988 (Scripture taken from THE HOLY BIBLE, NEW INTERNATIONAL VERSION, Copyright [symbol] 1973, 1978, 1984 International Bible Society. Used by permission of Zondervan Bible Publishers).

Unpublished stories, Deborah Sue Fordyce, 2000, 2011, 2017.

ACKNOWLEDGMENTS

KAREN LAFE, MY SISTER IN life, thanks for being there.

Clara Smith, adopted sister, for her love, dedication, and care for Mom and Dad and the family throughout the years.

Iliana Lara, owner of Casa de Angeles Assisted Living, for her devotion and friendship to Mom and Dad during their time at the Casa.

Virginia Smith, for her friendship and the loving medical care she provided as a hospice nurse.

Brian Turner, hospice chaplain, for his friendship and spiritual guidance.

"Born to be sisters" Karen and Debbie in the early 1950's.

"The foursome" Gene, Margaret, Karen and Debbie in 1950

"Daddy loves his girls" Gene, Karen and Debbie in the 1950's.

"A beautiful bride" Mom on her wedding day in 1941"

"Sweethearts" Mom and Dad in the early 1940's

Grandma Edna "Nanny" and Grandma Rachel
at Mom and Dad's wedding in 1941.

"Aging well" Mom and Dad in the 1990's

"Still sweethearts" Mom and Dad on 50th anniversary.

Dad loved the military life

"Aging gracefully together" Roy, Dad and Debbie

ABOUT THE AUTHOR

DEBBIE LAFE' FORDYCE IS RETIRED from the everyday workforce and currently resides in Arizona with her husband of more than fifty-three years. Debbie has two adult children, seven grandchildren, and one great-grandchild. She identifies herself as an ordinary person in the scheme of things.

While an avid reader, Debbie enjoys writing about both fiction and nonfiction relationships. Over the years, she has written both poetry and short stories that depict real-life faith, family, and values. Before Debbie retired, she wrote about military life from a child and teen viewpoint to assist her coworkers' understanding of their military clients. Now Debbie is sharing her first nonfiction book, *From Fishing to Tumbleweeds,* taking us through events which we all must eventually traverse.

CPSIA information can be obtained
at www.ICGtesting.com
Printed in the USA
BVHW050444130722
641931BV00002B/286

9 781685 704827